AF504328

A MISSIONARY'S LIFE
IN NYASALAND

A GROUP AT LIKOMA.

A MISSIONARY'S LIFE
IN NYASALAND

BY THE REV. G. H. WILSON, M.A.

Deus lo volt!

THE UNIVERSITIES' MISSION TO CENTRAL AFRICA
9 DARTMOUTH STREET, WESTMINSTER, S.W.1

Preface

THERE are some happy beings, no doubt of finer clay, who go through life with a serene confidence. They always seem to know the right course, as though by divine inspiration, and are never at a loss. With me things have been very different. Whenever I have had to make an important decision in my life, it has been made at the cost of a bitter inward struggle. More than ever in my life was this the case when I felt the first promptings to offer myself for missionary work. Was it my duty or was it not? I could not tell. Moreover, probably through my own dulness, I was quite unable to picture to myself what sort of life a missionary priest's might be. I felt that I ought to have some idea, for it seemed an important factor in solving the problem. Then I was lucky enough, though I ought not to call it luck, to come across Miss Gertrude Ward's inimitable letters. It was that book, I think, which led me to offer myself to The Universities' Mission to Central Africa. I am not so foolish as to think that I have Miss Ward's pen, but I would fain do something of the same sort for my own diocese. For this reason, after fifteen years of experience, I have made some attempt to draw a picture of our very happy life in the diocese of Nyasaland. It has been written at odd times, mostly at night. It must needs, therefore, be scrappy and uneven, and can have no literary merit. Such as it is, I offer it in the hope that it may help some one, who is in the same fix as I was, and who wants to know something of the actual life out here, before he sums up on the great question.

I should like to add that, though I have written entirely about my own Mission and Diocese, it is not because I selfishly disregard the interests of other Missions. I am trying to present a picture of a small part of the Mission field, well aware how small it is, because I happen to know about it. I do most earnestly sympathize with every effort to spread abroad the knowledge of the love of God in Christ in every land and in every race.

I have written from my own personal experience, with but little advice from others. Some, doubtless, will not agree with all that I have said. I alone am responsible for what is written. I alone must bear the blame for all that is amiss.

G. H. WILSON.

Mponda's.
June 8, 1920.

Contents

List of Illustrations

A MISSIONARY'S LIFE IN NYASALAND

I

The Country

THE diocese of Nyasaland nominally covers a very large area, but our work for the most part lies on, or not very far from, the great Lake Nyasa. The size of the lake generally comes as a surprise to English folk, accustomed to think in terms of our own Lakeland or, at most, of the Swiss Lakes. It is about 360 miles long—rather longer, in fact, than from Berwick-on-Tweed to Southampton—stretching roughly from the latitude 9°30′ to 14°30′ S. It is about sixty miles wide at the broadest part, but generally a good deal less. It forms a long strip of water running almost due north and south, except that about fifty miles from the southern end a broad arm stretches out towards the south-west to a distance of about forty-five miles from the main waters of the lake. The water is, of course, fresh, and in places it is very deep. It will be easily understood that such a large sheet of water is apt to become very rough at times (at least, for such small craft as ply on the lake up to the present). The strong wind is the south wind, called Mwela by the natives. This often blows with great violence in the cooler months, from May to the end of July, and sometimes for several days together. The other wind most dreaded by the natives is the north-wester, which often springs up with great suddenness in the early part of the rainy season. It comes with tremendous fury, but generally only lasts for a short time. Even in a short time it lashes the fresh water into angry waves, enough to be very dangerous for canoes. At other times the lake is more often calm than not, lying a lovely blue under the tropical sun. At night it is almost always calm, except when the Mwela is blowing. One can generally see the flares of the fishermen, often far out at sea, and one can often hear the peculiar signal for drawing the net, made by tapping the canoe with a paddle, carried a tremendous distance through the still night.

The Lake country seems to me to be extraordinarily beautiful. With the exception of a part of the western side, there are generally hills close to the shore. These are wooded, sometimes right down to the water's edge. It is impossible to describe the beauty of these woods, and they are so different from what I had expected a tropical forest to be. I thought to find enormous trees above, through which the sunlight could scarcely find its way, and below an impenetrable jungle. As a matter of fact, the trees are small but they are extraordinarily graceful in shape, while the undergrowth, though tiresome enough to walk through, is not very dense. Indeed, after the bush-fires, when the new grass is sprouting, one sees green glades of bright-looking turf such as one might find in an English park. Of course, there are bigger trees. There is the baobab, a sort of a hippo-potamus of a tree, of enormous bulk and quaint shape. Also in the river valleys magnificent timber trees are to be found, and very beautiful these valleys are. But it is the forest-clad hills that seem to me the most lovely. Crags of grey granite stand out, just as the limestone rocks do in my own Derbyshire hills. They stand always the same, or almost always, for in the rainy season one often sees glittering patches, where water trickles over them. But the forests themselves are always changing. I can never make up my mind at which season I love them best. In July and August the trees stand bare of leaves, of a delicate silver grey, except a sort of plane tree, whose white trunk stands out here and there in startling contrast. In the spring the forest shows every colour from the palest green, through orange and red, to purple. Even trees of the same species growing side by side put forth their new leaves of widely different colours. Then there are the dark, rich greens of summer, as beautiful again in another fashion. Lastly, autumn brings its amazing wonder of colour. Truly Africa is a fair place.

I am no naturalist, so I had better not attempt to describe the creatures that haunt these woods, yet even to an unscientific person they are intensely interesting. There are antelopes of all sizes, from the huge eland to the tiny klipspringer. There are elephants, though indeed I have never seen one. Often enough I have seen their tracks and the fearful devastation wrought where they have passed. There are birds of all colours, and some which sing quite passably, though they cannot equal the English nightingale or blackbird. There are dangerous beasts, too, both lions and leopards. Snakes also abound, a few dangerous, but mostly quite harmless. It must not be thought that these beasts are a great danger to Europeans. I have never heard, since I came into the country, of a European being hurt by a lion or a leopard, except when hunting them. With natives it is very different. They live in frail huts, they have no lamps to carry about at night, they often sleep out when on a journey, they have to watch their fields by night. There is a sad tale of natives killed by wild beasts every year. I have never heard in my time of a single person, native or European, dying of a snake bite. There are baboons and monkeys, platoons of them, wild dogs and pigs. There are butter-flies and other insects—ah me ! how many !—bats and lizards, an innumerable multitude of creatures. At night what sounds one hears when one camps in the forest ! One may hear the fateful note of the horned owl—bird of ill omen in native folklore—the appalling howl of the hyena, the curious treble pipe of the wild dog, the deep bass roar of the lion and countless other sounds, recognized and un-recognized, which tell of the teeming life of the forest. A naturalist would surely find this country an earthly paradise.

The climate of Nyasaland has been badly maligned, as it seems to me. To the feelings it is almost perfect. It is never desperately hot. The heat is seldom above 96° or 97° in the shade, though I have known it a good deal hotter. The cold is seldom below 52°. Oddly enough, this feels very cold, and a new-comer will be surprised to find how real is the need of thick clothes at times in this tropical country. I speak, however, of the lake-level. There have been frosts at Mtonya, and I have myself seen 111° in the shade at Port Herald.

I admit a strong dislike for the rainy season, but then I have a good deal of travelling about to do. Even then we have some sun most days, sometimes for many days, to the grievous destruction of crops. The rains are roughly from November to the end of April in the Lake district. Here at Mponda's thirty inches is not a bad fall. At Kota Kota they expect seventy inches. My last year at Likoma we had forty-five inches, which was a record fall up to that time. But the rain doesn't last very long, nor, as we have seen, does it rain all the time. It is merely a time when one expects rain, much as one expects rain almost at any time in England. Certainly, as far as feelings go, I would not wish for a better climate. Of course, there is malaria, but modern medical science has done wonders in prevention and also in curing us again when we do get fever. There are also other tropical diseases, such as dysentery. But my own opinion is—though I daresay it isn't worth much—that the real danger lies in the fact that somehow the country does take a good deal out of one. Maybe the food is not very nourishing, or perhaps we need " a brave north-easter " now and then. Anyway, most people get thin in Nyasaland and also most people get rather nervy, even though they escape all tropical diseases. That seems to me to be the reason why we should be rather more careful than we have been to refuse folks who are not reasonably strong. It is not fair on them or on the Mission to let them come out, and indeed break-downs have been too frequent in the past. But I don't believe that any normally healthy person has much to fear for his health's sake, if only he will not run foolish risks and will take reasonable precautions.

II

The People

THE district round Lake Nyasa is very thickly populated for Africa. Almost every little bay on the lake has its village, or even several villages. There is a succession of villages on the banks of the streams that flow into the lake, right up into the hills. Even streams which appear to run dry in the dry season often have their villages, and the village folk get water by digging deep pits in the apparently dry bed of the stream.

This population is made up of a large number of tribes. I could not possibly enumerate them myself, and if I could it would be unnecessary for our present purpose. It is perhaps better to consider those peoples with whom the Mission comes in contact according to their languages, for language in this country is not always a clue to the tribe. For instance, the Angoni (Zulu) have almost entirely dropped their own tongue and now talk a sort of Chi-Nyanja. The Mission works among four languages which, of course, are all dialects of the Bantu family. Far the largest part of our work lies among those speaking different forms of Chi-Nyanja, whom we may perhaps call Nyasas (Wa Nyanja), if we remember that it is a linguistic not a tribal name. To the south-east live Yaos, speaking Yao. I am inclined to think those who speak Yao are much more of one tribe than those who speak Chi-Nyanja, though I know small Yao-speaking villages whose folk call themselves Yaos, but who are not really of that tribe. Up north, in conquered German territory, we have two more dialects. I don't know what are their proper names. For convenience they are called by us Wa Manda and Wa Mpoto. Amongst one folk we have a large number of stations, amongst the others only four or five. Though I can give very little information about these Northerners, it is worth remembering that they are extraordinarily ready to receive Christianity, and their importance must not be judged by the scanty information that I can give. For the rest the ground is covered by Nyasas and Yaos.

There are certain things that are worth remembering about these two divisions. Speaking of them as we meet them, the Yaos are certainly the more advanced politically. They are organized in large divisions under great chiefs, though if the man who occupies the traditional position of the great chief happens for the moment to be a feeble person, the organization becomes very loose. Nyasas, on the contrary, are organized in separate villages. For instance, they would not be greatly moved if a neighbouring village were raided, except for feelings of natural pity or for fear that their own turn might come next. Hence, when Yaos and Nyasas have clashed, the Yaos have been generally victorious, for obviously the large tribe has an overwhelming advantage over the single village. Certainly this shows the political superiority of the Yaos, though I doubt if it necessarily proves the personal superiority often claimed by Yao admirers. Also, once in my knowledge, Nyasas, fighting Yaos on equal terms, were completely victorious. On the other hand, I think that Nyasa morals are unquestionably higher than those of the Yaos, but this may be owing to the effect of a low type of Islam. Of this I shall hope to speak later. Here one may note that Nyasas are mostly heathen and Yaos are in the main Moslems —that is, of course, where they have not yet accepted Christianity.

Having mentioned these differences, I shall now speak of the general characteristics which are met with in both peoples, for to a great extent they are the same. Now I hear people say sometimes that they can distinguish at once between a Nyasa and a Yao by their appearance. I should very much like to test this claim. I admit readily that there is a difference, but I could not myself undertake to distinguish at sight between a Nyasa and a Yao, except in rare cases where the difference was very marked. It is often amusing, too, to hear Europeans, both missionaries and others, claiming that the tribe amongst whom their lot is cast is far the superior. I have lived and worked among both and, if I live another year, I shall have spent an equal length of time amongst each people. I still cannot tell the difference between them at sight, and I am still at a loss to know which of the two I like best.

These people are not black, but a sort of chocolate colour. One good priest of our Mission used to tell his cook to roast coffee beans till they became not black but the colour of his own arm—a very sound maxim for roasting coffee, and the reader will see at once the colour of the cook. I think myself there is a great deal to be said for the colour. In children it is really beautiful. In adults, too, it will bear comparison with our own pale faces, for a European complexion does not look its best in Central Africa. I never realized this till my first trip home. I remember standing amazed at the beauty of the complexion of the Southampton dock-hands—not generally, I suppose, regarded as a high type of English complexion! The natives almost always have soft, brown eyes. Our greys and greens seem inexpressibly fierce to them. I admit that the nose and lips are hard to defend, but in spite of this I have certainly seen beautiful faces amongst them, and some even noble. To me the African face is generally very attractive. They have beautifully white teeth and a charming grin, and have also an open air of frankness which is very engaging, an air which is conspicuously lacking among the Eastern peoples. If this frank air makes the simple new-comer think that the African is but a shallow person, easy to be understood, he will find himself grievously mistaken. The African is simply a born actor, indeed I think he is acting most of the time, sometimes I fear with real intention to deceive, more often in naïve unconsciousness. In figure the African is often magnificent. He is not very tall, shorter a good deal on an average than the Englishman, but he is commonly beautifully built. The women, especially the young ones, carry themselves splendidly, sometimes with a load on their heads and a baby on their backs. Some people tell me that they find the African repulsive. I cannot understand that myself.

I think it must be some unconscious prejudice
at the back of their mind. For my own
part, from the very first I felt a great attraction towards the Africans of Nyasaland.

When one comes to consider the character
of these folk I think that again one must admit
that they are a very lovable people. Of course,
I don't mean that their character is perfect,
far from it, but when one fairly considers their
opportunities I think they will bear favourable
comparison with other races. I do not pretend
to give an analysis of African character, that
would indeed be a rash thing to do, but one
cannot live many years amongst people of
another race without acquiring certain definite
ideas about them. I give these for what they
are worth. At least they may be found interesting, and I should like to think that some of
my readers may some day have an opportunity
of correcting my impressions by their own
experience.

There seem to me to be two special failings
in the African character which constantly show
themselves. I will mention these first and be
done with them. In the first place the African
seems to lack something, some stiffness of
character, some backbone—I do not know what
to call it. This is often very exasperating to
an Englishman, for it makes some of the best
Africans fail one just when one least expects

it. It is not that they lose their heads at a crisis. Some do, of course, but I have myself seen a native show splendid presence of mind in moments of difficulty and also of danger. It is not that they lack staying power. Can any one who has travelled in Central Africa ever forget his carriers, weary, patient and enduring ? The pathos of it ! Perhaps an example will best show what I mean. My teacher is a good fellow and has a real zeal for his work—I speak generically—but if he happens to feel unwell in the morning he simply drops everything. He has certain quite important duties to do, but he just lets them go. He does not live fifty yards away, yet he would not think of sending me a message. I should probably find out before school-time, but if I did not there would be no bell and no school. Nor could he be brought to see that he was in the least blameworthy. This, of course, is not a very serious case, but I fear it would be just the same where really important issues were involved. Then think of the contrast. The European, in the first instance, would generally fight against his illness as long as he could. When obliged to give in he would try his best to arrange so as not to leave all his work in confusion. I suppose our religion and civilization have ground into us the importance of duty, while the African does not as yet feel a very strong sense of duty.

No doubt he will improve, but at present, even in some of the best, men whom I regard as real friends, I fancy I see traces of this lack, whatever it be.

The second failing comes as a shock to one. At first one is greatly struck by the honest expression of the African face. As a matter of fact dishonesty, in word and deed, is a notable characteristic of the Central African folk.* I say this very sadly, but with deep conviction. In village life I do not believe that there is any disgrace attached to dishonesty, unless it be found out. I am not speaking so much of the relations between Africans and Europeans, though there it is distressing enough. But still one can admit some excuse. We seem inordinately rich and also selfish, and moreover the climate tries the temper. I do not think it seems very wrong to a native to help himself to our superfluous wealth, which seems to him selfishly hoarded. Nor do I think it unnatural that they should use deceit to avoid or appease our fierce wrath. What really hurts me is the plundering of some poor old widow's field, the sneaking of hardly earned coppers from a companion in the dormitory, the robbing of some poor traveller. In a native court lying is carried to a fine art. It

* This statement would not be endorsed by every one in the U.M.C.A.—Publishers.

is a disgrace to give away your own side by
speaking the truth. It is as bad as for an
English public school boy to sneak. However,
one hopes that Christianity will alter this.
Indeed it is doing so, but slowly, I am sorry to
say. I fear it cannot be disputed that this is a
marked trait of Africans in general, though
one is thankful to have known many who
are exceptions, the more honour to them.

We have told the worst, and even these
bad traits could be paralleled among many
so-called higher races. No doubt, too, there
are many other faults, such as are found in
other peoples, immorality, drunkenness and
such like. Where are they not found ? But
when one has said all this, I am still convinced
that the natives of Central Africa are a most
lovable people. Let us now consider their
good points.

The first thing that strikes one is their
cheerfulness. They don't seem to have too
much to make them cheerful, but they make
the best of things. They live almost entirely
in the present, so that when all is well they are
full of careless happiness. Perhaps because
they are so thoughtless they are soon cast down.
In sickness, as we saw before, they collapse.
A death in the village casts a shadow over the
whole place. Travellers who hurry through
Africa speak as if a native's life was a supremely

happy one. I do not think it is at all, but they make the best of it, and it is a very good trait in their character. Your passing traveller does not see much of the seamy side of native life. How should he?

Perhaps connected with their happy disposition is their extraordinary good temper. It is true that, when once roused, the African temper rises almost to a frenzy. Indeed that may be partly why he has had to learn to keep it under control, unless greatly exasperated, for village custom demands heavy damages for blows, heavier still if blood flow. Even if this be so to some extent, I am sure that they are also naturally good-tempered. I have often watched boys playing football, and in dead earnestness too, but I have very seldom seen any one lose his temper. In this large and somewhat unruly village how seldom there is a serious fight! Even then it is nearly always caused by drink. There is incomparably less quarrelling here than in some of our slums at home.

Africans, too, are extraordinarily ready to forgive, as soon as their momentary indignation has passed off. It is astonishing how they forgive us Europeans our blunders and mistakes. I do not often whip a boy, but for one or two serious offences a whipping is the recognized punishment. It is the last thing, short of expulsion. I once whipped a boy for a flagrant offence. Soon after his complete innocence was suddenly established by a strange chain of coincidences. I at once apologized and gave him a present to show my regret. Indeed I made all possible amends, for I was horribly ashamed of myself. Now I don't believe the boy ever bore me a moment's ill will. He knew that I was acting justly, as far as I could see, and he seemed to think it rather splendid of me to own up and make amends. He forgave me readily enough. It was not nearly so easy for me to forgive myself.

Unselfishness is another splendid trait in the African character. If you give some sugar or salt to a boy, he shares round to the last grain. " The man who eats alone " is a proverbial term of contempt. In native eyes we seem fearfully selfish. If you have some cigarettes and smoke one, keeping the rest by you, when you know that all around would like one, it seems almost brutal. You might at least pass round the lighted one for all to have a suck ! The African is really unselfish and feels the keenest shame if he has been betrayed into an act of selfishness. A woman once came to me in the greatest distress, for she felt that she had committed an appalling sin. She had refused a traveller water, who came to her house to beg a drink as he passed by. I may say that she has to fetch every drop of water from quite a distance in a great earthen pitcher, which she carries on her head. There was no doubt at all that the poor woman was really overwhelmed with the sense of shame. It is true that she was not a raw native. She was a Christian and one of the best. Now I wonder how many European Christians would have felt the sting of conscience for driving a tramp from the door, even though they had but to turn a tap to satisfy his wants.

I think far the most striking point in the African character is their family affection. It is simply wonderful and naively taken for granted. They stand by one another through thick and thin, at home and abroad. When separated they love to write and receive letters. They will go long journeys to see a distant kinsman, especially if he be ill. This affection is not limited to one small family circle, but it extends to kinsfolk so distant that we find it hard to express the relationship. Death makes an appalling breach in the circle. The wailing after a death is a dreadful sound and, for the time at least, the sorrow is genuine. I admit that so thoughtless a people soon forget, but that is only what one would expect. They love their children just as much as we do, possibly more. This intense love often shows itself in an unfortunate way, for they seldom correct small children and they are apt to get spoilt. Often enough I have pressed a woman to insist on an urchin of seven or eight coming to school. She replies in despair, " But he refuses," as if that settled the question. They love them too much to punish their children, but, though they are unwise, it is real love. A friend of mine was once speaking to a native who had just returned from the Somali campaign. He had been serving in the King's African Rifles. My friend expected him to enlarge on such things as big guns and maxims and those sort of horrors, which must have been a terrible experience to a village lad. But the horror that seemed most to dwell in his mind was that he had seen Somali women fleeing from the enemy, who threw their babies away into the bush in their terror. That seemed to him the accursed thing. He added, as a very natural corollary, " But we beat them and made them take them up again." All through the village relationships, it is the family which counts ; the individual is only important as one of the family. If a lad is earning wages, it is to a large extent for the family, and he is expected to share round, and he admits the claim. One must remember, however, that the family is not constituted like ours. The father is outside. He has no rights in the children. They belong to the mother's family. Native custom makes the most careful provision for the protection of the mother and children in the interests of their family. Inheritance goes not to a man's own son, but to his sister's son; that is, it remains in the family and does not pass to the mother's family, according to native ideas. But though the family be differently constituted, the family tie is real enough and it is enormously stronger than the ordinary family tie in Europe. Christianity is rapidly changing the organization of the family. It is possible that it may for a time weaken its force, where the Christianity is not very sincere, but ,I have not noticed a sign of this. It merely seems to bring the father into the circle, who was before outside.

There is one fact which, as an Englishman, I take great pride in telling. During the whole Central African campaign in the late war, whatever happened, none of the 1st King's African Rifles (our Nyasaland battalions) ever ran away. In ordinary life natives are ready enough to run away, especially when they see no particular reason for standing their ground, but I always felt that there was real courage behind. When trained by British officers, as all military men tell me, they made magnificent soldiers. This is not only true of the old 1st/1st, a splendidly disciplined regiment, but it is equally true of the newer second battalion and also of the latest raised third.   All honour to them and to their officers who led them !

III

The Village

THE centre of African life is the village. A European has to get away from his conception of a village as a place where so many folks happen to dwell, because of work or inclination or what not, and from this mere fact of dwelling together, become an organized community. In Africa the village is the home of a clan, together with its slaves. We commonly speak of slaves, but I think it would be more proper to call them "serfs." If the clan is large, parts of it may live in different actual localities, but in native eyes it is one village. It is quite common round Mponda's for a village to be divided into two or three parts. Part of Malunga's village live by the lake and part in the hills, twenty miles away, but both parts together make up Bolela—the village name. Hence to live, as folk live at home, amongst strangers, perhaps not even known by name, is simply inexplicable to a native—it is more, it is horrible and unnatural.

The village is like a large family, of which the chief is father and he rules in patriarchal fashion over it. The slaves are the property of the family. They have generally come into the family either as prisoners of war or as payment for some crime. This cannot happen now under British rule, so there are only the descendants of slaves. I don't think slaves are ever sold now. A few years ago a big Yao chief in the Portuguese hills sent a present of a slave wife to a chief in these parts. That is the nearest approach to slave-dealing that I have met myself, and that was so unusual that it caused a tremendous sensation. I speak with caution, for it is difficult to be certain, but I don't think these slaves are badly used, on the whole. Of course, they are still slaves and have no part in the village politics. It may seem strange to English ears to hear that there are still slaves under the British flag. It is quite true that any slave may go before the magistrate and claim his freedom. If he knows his own ancestral clan, certainly he can go there and live as a free man. Even then, if it were too near, it might be dangerous. If he does not know his own folks, he is at a standstill. He cannot go and live in another village. He would merely become the slave of new masters in another clan. An African without a village is one of the most desolate creatures on earth. If he has no folk of his own, his only niche in society, such as it is, is his position of slave in the village of his masters, and he had far better stay there. Things, however, are changing. I suppose he might now make his way to South Africa and begin life afresh in one of those native conglomerations near some large town.

The village[1] is generally a picturesque object. From the lake one sees a bright stretch of sand in some bay or other convenient spot, behind which there lies a collection of huts. A few of larger size will stand out, the huts of the leading mèn of the community. One of these will be the chief's. Generally a shady tree has been left near the chief's house, or he has built his house purposely near to one. There he holds his court. Also the village dances and other public functions are held there. It is the "agora" or "forum" of the African village. On the sand just clear of the water there will be two or three dug-out canoes. Above again it is likely that a large fishing-net is spread out. This is the common property of the village, and men are generally to be seen mending such rents as have been made during the last night's fishing. Still higher up, almost

[1] I have described a lake-side village. An inland village is much the same if you take away the canoes and fishing nets.

among the huts, there is generally a shelter,
just a thatched roof standing on poles. Under
the shadow of this shelter one sees a few old
men, twisting fibre into string (by rubbing
it on their thighs) for mending the net, or for
making a new one. Behind the huts lies the
village field and behind that again the forest.
Sometimes the forest is close behind the village,
and then you must seek the village field farther
away. All around the great common field,
at the edge of the forest, are little thatched
shelters. They are generally placed on higher
ground, perhaps on an old ant-hill, so as to
command a view. Often they are raised on
poles, as much as 10 or 12 feet. Night and day
the fields must be watched, from the sowing,
in November or December, until the maize
is safely stored at the end of May. Baboons
and monkeys are ever on the watch to sneak
in by day. Wild pigs may swarm in by night.
Then as the grain forms and ripens, birds must
be scared away. One day or one night may
be long enough to destroy most of the crop,
if the villagers neglect to watch. The principal
crop is the maize. There is also millet, sometimes running nearly up to 20 feet. This is
eaten in porridge and is often used to make gruel
for the sick, but its main purpose is for brewing
beer. If there be a marshy spot, there will also
be rice. Between the maize stalks, beans and

A LAKESIDE VILLAGE,

pumpkins of many sorts are grown. Monkey-nuts have a patch all to themselves.

The houses are built of poles, sunk into the ground and about 18 inches apart. Between them the space is filled in with reeds, or sometimes millet stalks or even strong grass. The whole is generally plastered over with ant-mud, within and without. The floor, too, and the space under the eaves is also mudded. The roof is thatched with grass, and the eaves hang over, making a sort of verandah. Some houses are round and some oblong, but the chief's is generally oblong in these parts. Behind is a courtyard, shut in with a grass fence, for the sake of privacy. Here the woman generally does her pounding, and often the cooking, too. There is little furniture within. There are sleeping mats, often a bedstead—just a wooden frame tightly strung with palm-leaf ropes and exceedingly comfortable. There are also pitchers and an earthen cooking-pot and various baskets. There is a hoe and an axe, with a very narrow blade. In the lakeside villages, or in a village near a large stream, there will be small nets and a fish trap. This last is a really clever piece of work, made of split bamboo. In the courtyard is the inevitable mortar, for pounding maize, fashioned out of the bole of a tree, together with two or three heavy pestles.

The most important question in village life is the food supply. Work is begun in the fields in September or even earlier. The ground has to be cleared of weeds first. The Yao villages in the hills change their fields every few years. If it is very far, the whole village moves too. They then ruthlessly cut down acres of beautiful trees. They use what they want for building purposes and firewood, and pile the rest in heaps and burn it. This is a tremendous undertaking with their tiny axes, and they often begin operations before the harvest in the previous year. As soon as the rains are thought to have begun in earnest the seed is sown, it may be in November, but more generally in December. When the rains are very late they may not be able to sow until January. When the corn is getting ripe, the old store-houses are repaired and new ones built. They look rather like little huts on short legs. The roof is movable and can be lifted off to get out the contents, and there is a rough ladder attached. Then comes the harvest. Up till now, both men and women share in the work. Now it is the women who carry the maize home in large baskets and pour it into the store. Thenceforth it is in the woman's charge. No man may venture to go to the store to help himself. Custom absolutely forbids it. An offended lady may refuse supplies

to her lord for days, and, if he has only one lady,
he is in a sorry plight. It is the woman who
takes the grain out of the store, puts it to soak
and ferment for several days, then dries it on
a mat in the sun and afterwards pounds it
in the mortar, and finally prepares the porridge.
On Likoma this porridge is generally made of
cassava, treated in much the same way. With
this porridge a relish is eaten, beans or fish
or, on very rare occasion, meat. In the lake-
side villages it is the men's business to provide
fish. Whenever the weather is fit, some of the
men spend part of the night fishing. Sometimes
small private nets are used, but more often the
big common net of the village. In that case
the chief, or one of the head-men, divides the
catch. When the food is cooked, the men eat
first by themselves, afterwards the women.
A boy new to table work is amazed at our
custom of helping the ladies first. He is
equally amazed that we leave food uneaten
on the table. One meal a day in the evening
is the usual custom in the village. That should
be porridge. It is not a meal if there is not
porridge. At the same time, when they may
be come at, other things are often eaten between
times, such as maize or monkey-nuts, roasted
casually over a fire of grass or what not. Folks
often go about gnawing sugar cane, or the sweet
stalk of the millet. Just before the harvest,

everybody is munching green corn, and grievous pains in the middle prostrate youngsters on all hands.

But the regular supply of food is often interrupted by some mischance befalling the fields. As has been seen above, the beasts of the forest may cause great havoc. Besides baboons, monkeys and pigs, there are the bigger game. Herds of buck may do much mischief. Elephants are especially dreaded. Not only will they invade the gardens, but they will come into the village and overset the stores, as happened close to us here about a month ago. The villagers told me that they lit flares of grass and beat tin cans, but the elephants took not the least notice. But the weather is the worst danger. A spell of dry weather in the rainy season, when the crops are young, is disastrous. Or too heavy rain may wash whole gardens away. Every year brings the villagers face to face with this anxiety. It must be remembered that there is no means of importing food, and it is impossible to save surplus stock for long in their primitive stores. Even though there may be plenty of food in a neighbouring district, transport is so difficult that it is hard to keep up the supply in the area of scarcity. Practically the only means of transport is by carrier. Last year one saw on the roads an unending stream of weary

men and women, carrying loads of food from
the district round Lake Malombe to the hungry
villages in this neighbourhood.

The politics of the village are simple. The
chief is the centre of authority, and behind him
are the head-men. The chief is not the son of
his predecessor, but his sister's son. There are
generally more than one in the right relationship and then the village chooses. They seem
to follow the old Anglo-Saxon custom of
choosing the ablest man of the royal race—
though the royal race is reckoned on a different
principle. Of legislation there is little. There
are temporary orders, but they, in a small way,
rather resemble our orders-in-council. A recognized body of custom takes the place of the
law. This is very complicated and covers
every possible contingency in life. It is absolutely binding. I never yet heard of a man
venturing to defy custom. Hence the chief's
duty, as a judge, is to decide questions in his
court according to custom. Each side tries to
prove that he has custom on his side. If he
succeeds, that settles the question. A native
court is really a very wonderful thing. Each
side has its spokesman, who takes the place of
our barrister, and wonderful orators they are.
Witnesses are not separated, but give evidence
as they are called. First one spokesman
explains his case and then the other, but that

is not the end. They go on in turn, sometimes for hours, until at last they agree that they have had "enough words." Then the chief takes one of the orators in hand and questions him very rapidly, taking him through his case with a running fire of questions, which only need an answer of yes or no. Sometimes it is not the chief himself who questions. He may depute one of his head-men who are sitting with him. They are extraordinarily clever in questioning and, if there be anything shady in the case, it generally comes out, upon which the opposition laugh with intention in high glee. Then comes the opposition's turn, and the other side marks the discrepancies with derisive laughter. Finally the chief, or the head-man deputed by him, sums up and gives judgment.

I cannot say how far custom is apt to change in normal times. During the war the whole system of village life was brought into sharp contact with European civilization and no doubt the shock was tremendous. Wherever a European goes he seems to carry some subtle power of change. Whether it be the government official, the missionary, the planter or the trader—each is working for change, whether he knows it or not. It is too early to assess the effect of the war, but at least it must mean an enormous amount of change. I feel that the whole present condition of native life is likely to be radically affected in the next few years. This is a matter of great anxiety to all who love Africans, for I cannot feel at all certain that this change must necessarily be for the better.

IV

The Diocese

THE history of the diocese can be read in
the general history of the Mission. One
may, perhaps, just mention the principal facts,
for convenience. Our first missionaries, though
they aimed at settling on the lake, never got
there and finally failed to establish themselves
in the Shiré Highlands or at Morambala. It is
a tragic story of a splendid struggle against
tropical disease at a time when medical science
could not give very much help. Bishop Tozer
had to withdraw to Zanzibar, at that time
the centre towards which all East African
interests tended. His eyes were still turned
towards the lake, but meanwhile it was hoped
that the missionaries might get more experience
to fight the climate, and also might learn something of the languages of the interior amongst
the crowds of strangers and slaves in Zanzibar.
Bishop Steere once more planned an advance
to the lake. Archdeacon Johnson and Mr.

Janson were his messengers. I wish Archdeacon Johnson could be persuaded to write the history of those days. They arrived in 1882 at the lake and since then the work has gradually grown. In 1895 Nyasaland and Zanzibar became separate dioceses, each having its own bishop.

The head-quarters of the diocese are at Likoma Island about half-way up the lake. Here is the Cathedral Church, and the Bishop has his permanent home there, though much of his time is necessarily spent in travelling about his diocese. The doctor also has his head-quarters at Likoma and the central store of the medical department. The diocesan library and the printing press are naturally at head-quarters. At the north end of the island, at Makalawe, St. Michael's Training College for teachers is now permanently established. St. Andrew's Theological College is at the opposite end, at Nkwazi, but during the war the college had to be closed. Likoma Island is a station apart. One has every reason to hope that in a few years it will be altogether a Christian island. Though the head-quarters of the Mission are at Likoma, the treasurer and the general store are at Mponda's, as being more nearly in touch with the outside world. The engineering shop is at Malindi, which thus becomes the head-quarters of the steamers. There is to be an engineer permanently in charge of this shop for the future.

The principle on which the diocese is organized is to have a number of head-stations, from each of which a large district is worked. Before the war the s.s. *Chauncy Maples*, and before her the s.s. *Charles Janson*, were practically movable head-stations, from which a large district was worked along the lake shore and, in some cases, stretching far inland. When the war broke out, the steamers were commandeered, and after that the *Chauncy Maples* was under repairs. The steamer district is to be divided, for it had grown to unmanageable proportions. In the districts worked from the head-station or steamer are a number of sub-stations. Each of these is provided with a resident teacher. He conducts the school, teaches the hearers and catechumens, takes services on Sunday and short prayers on week-days, and generally presides over the Christian community, often a very small one. It is his business also to keep in touch with the villagers, to encourage the children to come to school and to influence the elders, as far as possible, to listen to the Christian message.

It will be seen at once that these native teachers play a very important part in our work. They are selected from the most promis-

THE S.S. "CHAUNCY MAPLES" AT OLD LANGENBERG.

ing boys in the different schools. They must pass an entrance examination before entering college, which is an intellectual test, and they must have the recommendation of their priest-in-charge, which means that he has assured himself that the boy is one who may be reasonably expected to show the right moral qualities of a teacher. They then enter St. Michael's College, where they have 'a course of three years, with a break of a year at the end of the second year in residence. During the year's break they are put under some experienced teacher, so as to learn the practical part of the work, before going back for their last year at college. Every effort is made to imbue these students with a right spirit, for their work is to a large extent ministerial work. The chapel is the centre of the college, and their work as messengers of the gospel is kept continually in view. When the teacher leaves college with his final certificate he is set to work, at first generally under an older teacher. When he is married he can be put in charge of an out-station. It is unfortunately quite impossible to put an unmarried boy or even a widower to live alone in charge of an out-station. There would always be danger, but apart from that, native custom makes it all but impossible. It has been seen above that the food is the woman's business. It is most improper for a woman to cook food for a man who is not her husband or a near kinsman. An unmarried teacher can only be put with another teacher, whose wife can cook for both, and if they eat together there is no scandal. It is from the teacher class that we look for our future ministry. We have already seven native priests and two deacons, besides a number of senior teachers, commissioned as readers or evangelists.

The diocese, with all its organizations, is for one purpose, the evangelization of the native Africans, so it may be well here to say something of the religion of the people to whom we preach. The work of the diocese is divided sharply into two very different kinds. In some parts we are preaching to heathen, in others to Mohammedans. As I have said before, the Nyasas are mostly heathen and the Yaos mostly Moslems. This is only a rough division, for there is a good deal of Islam amongst the Nyasas at Kota Kota and in the Monkey Bay district and farther south. There are also exceptions among the Yaos, but they are much more insignificant.

I have found it very difficult to learn anything very definite about the beliefs of the heathen. I am inclined to think that they are rather vague themselves, though a heathen native would be apt to be reserved about his

religion when speaking to a mission "padre."
Certainly they believe in a supreme God, perhaps
in one God, but it is difficult to be quite sure
of the latter statement, for they certainly believe
in evil spirits in a way which reminds one of the
dæmons or lesser gods of Greek mythology.
Still one is on solid ground when one starts
from their belief in a supreme God. Their
relations with God seem to consist mostly of
deprecation. To escape misfortune, bodily and
spiritual, is their chief concern. They believe
that spirits live on after death in the form of
ghosts, and they are horribly afraid of them.
I doubt if the native worries himself much
about the future. As in material things, he
lives in the present. Death is so very appalling
to him that he puts all thoughts of it as far
away as may be. It is of ill omen to use the
word. Used carelessly it may involve a curse.
Children are often called by names in which
the word death is found, such as " Little
death," " He dies to-morrow," or " He dies
for nothing." I think that this is done under
the idea of avoiding evil by affecting to expect
it. No one who has ever heard the wailing
after a death in the village can doubt that it
brings dismay and horror to the survivors as
well as grief. One may say, it seems to me,
that the religion of the heathen consists of a
vague belief in a supreme God and a multi-

tude of evil spirits, and an anxious desire to escape ill by means of charms and propitiatory invocations.   Beyond this one must add a vague idea of survival in a spirit world beyond the grave.

With Islam all is different.   Their beliefs are definite enough theoretically.   I am apt to doubt how far these professed beliefs have really sunk into the native mind.   It is the custom to rail at Islam and the reasons are obvious, but I must confess that to me it seems for men a distinct step up from heathenism. Even in its debased form, as we see it here, it does produce some characters who command our respect.   And it is a very debased form which we meet in Nyasaland.   Mostly folks are very ignorant about Moslem doctrines.   I have more than once asked a village Moslem teacher to read his prayer-board for me, and he has done so, tracing his finger from left to right. I can't read Arabic myself, but I know it runs the other way.   Rammadan is observed and folks even fast to some extent.   All join in the excitement, when Rammadan is over.   Prayers are said in the mosques, especially on Fridays and in Rammadan.   There is a mosque in most of the villages in these parts, generally a tiny reed-and-pole hut.   The Koran rules about intoxicants seem to be quite ignored.   The women take a distinct share in the worship at the mosque, which is good, but rather surprising, when one considers the position which they hold. Somehow Islam has got into the position of a native religion, while Christianity is distinctly regarded as European and foreign. I don't know whether it is by chance that Moslems have got into this position or by craft, but it is a disaster of the greatest moment to missionaries. For when I admitted that Islam is a step up, I mean that it is an isolated step, not a step on a ladder. It blocks the way to anything higher. Also, though it produces some fine characters, it has had a sadly bad effect on general morals. With the heathen a marriage is a breakable contract, but divorce is a very serious business. The parties must appear before the village court. Damages are assessed. Finally a reed is split down the middle before the assembly, and then the union is dissolved. A Moslem may tell his wife to go at any moment, and that is the end of the union. The result is that the marriage tie is appallingly slight. Folks change their partners continually, and just such a degradation of morals follows as one would expect. For the women especially this state of things is disastrous. Their standard of morals is very much lower than that of the heathen women and, what is worse, they seem quite content with it and to have no higher aspirations. One would have expected that the women would have resented bitterly being treated as chattels and dismissed at pleasure, but they do not seem to do so. Islam, such as it is, has a great attraction for Africans. Partly, as we have seen above, it comes to them as an African religion for Africans, which alone gives it a tremendous power. Then undoubtedly it does give a heathen more intelligent and definite relations with God. It teaches that the one great God does really rule and does care for his people, at least for Mohammedans. It is attractive, too, to human frailty in that it makes no great demands and is able to effect a compromise with existing customs in a way which Christianity cannot do. It allows a low moral tone and gives religious sanction to it. This means a great deal to a race which has never learnt to practise self-control or even to regard it as a virtue to be desired. Here, too, where the connexion with Zanzibar and the coast is still remembered, it gives a man an appreciable social lift. This does, perhaps, help a little towards self-respect, but it also ministers to a very sour kind of spiritual pride. It will easily be seen that Islam is a very serious enemy to Christianity. I have tried to speak fairly of it and to recognize such merits as it has, but as a Christian missionary I regret the spread of Islam very much. It is at most but a step up from heathenism, and as a stumbling-block to any further advance, especially towards Christianity, its influence is simply deplorable.

In the religion of the non-Christian natives, both Moslem and heathen, there are two points which any one, who has tried to understand them, must have noticed.

The first point is that they seem to lack a sense of sin. Perhaps this does not quite express what I mean, for natives are extraordinarily ready to confess a fault, if one can only keep one's own quick European temper under control and deal kindly and patiently with them. What I mean is that they have no sense of guilt for past sin. They do not seem to feel that anything is seriously wrong with themselves. There is none of that haunting conviction that something is vitally wrong with men, which was such a striking feature in the Græco-Roman world in the first days of the Church, a conviction that makes a man welcome the idea of redemption. An appeal to such a feeling leaves a native quite cold. That much is wrong with external things he is quick to recognize, but he does not realize at all how much is wrong with himself. Any one will see at a glance that this makes the missionary's work very hard. It is not on this point that one can find any leverage to lift the native from his present position.

The second point is this. Whatever Islam may teach, the old superstitions linger on, as they do in the Church to some extent, and I am persuaded that the chief factor in native religion, whether Moslem or heathen, is fear. All their lives they stand in deadly fear of charms and witchcraft. To them these things are terribly real. I learnt only the other day that a Moslem here has been driven from his village, because his boy was taken by a crocodile and he is supposed to have had some occult part in it. I had another striking instance of the reality of their belief in witchcraft. Soon after I left Likoma five canoes started to cross over to the western side of the lake. They were overtaken by a storm and two canoes were lost and twenty-two people drowned. I wrote a word of sympathy to the old chief, for he was rather a friend of mine. He wrote back, or rather he got some one else to write for him, for of course he cannot write himself, telling me all about the disaster and the names of his people who were drowned. Then he said, " And we know who did it. We went to the magistrate at Chinteche to bring a case against them. But he said, ' It is the hand of God, there is no case.' But (nampo kaya) that is as it may be." Now that old man is as sure that his enemies caused that storm by witchcraft as we are that two and two make four. There is another form of witchcraft which causes unspeakable terror. There is supposed to be a secret society, and I believe there is, who dig up dead bodies and are said to perform the most ghastly rites. These people are credited with fearful powers. Again, as we have seen above, there is always anxiety about food. A failure of the rains means famine. Now it is held that there are evil-disposed persons who can prevent the rain by secret practices. Moreover wild beasts are a really serious danger, but superstition adds further horrors. No non-Christian native doubts that it is possible for a man to assume the form of a wild beast, just as the old Anglo-Saxons believed in werwolves. Now I am not particularly fond of having a man-eating lion about the place myself, but just think what it would be if I thought that this lion was after me, endowed with all the cunning and malice of some special enemy. It is amusing to see natives jump, startled at some sudden noise, but at the same time to me it is unspeakably pathetic, for it seems to tell of the age-long reign of terror under which they and their ancestors have lived. It is this terror that seems to me to be at the bottom of all their charms and incantations, and to be the main factor in whatever religion they have.

V

The Station

THE head-station is the home of us European workers. It is astonishing how one gets attached to one's station. We are all quite sure that our own is the best and dislike moving to another very much. Though, when we do move, we soon find that after all our new station is the best. The regular staff for each station, according to the Bishop's scheme, consists of the priest-in-charge, a layman, a nurse and a lady teacher. Where the work is larger this minimum staff must be augmented. In others, alas, at present it falls short. Any one who knows anything of our work will see at once that the Bishop is right when he says that this ought to be the minimum staff on every head-station.

We live almost a family life. Each one of us has our own separate house. It is built of brick or stone and consists of two rooms. There is a common dining-room, where we take all our meals together. This seems an admirable plan.

It is not only a great saving of expense, but insures cheerful, social meals, which prevents one from getting too much wrapped up in the cares of one's work. Unfortunately it has one drawback, for it means a great deal of work for the housekeeper, generally the nurse, who has already more than enough to do. To run the housekeeping successfully and economically is no easy task. It is just one of those side-shows in missionary life which are but little noticed, and yet we owe a tremendous debt to those who unceasingly attend to our wants. It is of great importance to health in this exacting country to have our simple meals well cooked and nicely served. The cook and table-boys can turn out quite a successful meal, but they need constantly looking after. When this is done native table-boys are very deft and attentive, if not flurried.

At most of our stations the dining-room is in some central position. The ladies' houses are on one side, and somewhere within reach are the girls' dormitory, the girls' school and the women's hospital. The church is generally a little to itself, for it is obvious that one does not want a general congregation dispersing through the European part of the station or through the women's quarters. On the other side are the men's houses, the boys' dormitory and school, the teacher's house and the men's hospital. A spare house for native travellers is also a necessity, for Christians passing through naturally come to the Mission to sleep. The surgery is, if possible, somewhere between the two hospitals. I hope to say something about the medical work later. The dormitories are a feature of station life which needs explanation. All the pupils of our schools feed at home, with few exceptions. At present I have only three feeding on this station. One is a boy from a distance, who is learning the surgery work and two are cripples, cast off by their own kinsfolk. But all Christians and catechumen boys sleep on the station. In the village no unmarried boy sleeps at home with his parents. As early as at the age of six or seven they have to turn out. They sleep in common houses, unmarried men of all ages, and, as may be supposed, these bachelor houses are often not very desirable places. We follow the native custom, but insist that our Christian and catechumen boys should sleep in a common house or dormitory on the station, away at least from the worst temptations of village life. One can do a good deal in the way of securing decency and we have regular prayers for the boys, which no doubt are a great help. It is not quite the same with the girls, though they, too, have sometimes common houses. They generally, however, sleep· in a sort of out-house annexed to their parents' hut.

Here, and I think at most big stations, it is found best that the Christian and catechumen girls should sleep in a dormitory on the station, under the care of one of the ladies. We have boys' dormitories in the same way at our out-stations, but I have never ventured on a girls' dormitory. Teachers change and go for holidays, so at times there would be no supervision, and in any case the responsibility is more than I dare undertake.

The schools form a very important part of our work. In all times missionaries have done well to get hold of the children. It is a great thing if the teacher has the gift of making school bright and interesting, for, unless a child's parents are Christians, one can exert very little pressure to induce children to come. It is a source of wonder to me that they come as well as they do. We teach the three R's and just a smattering of English. The top classes are rather more advanced, for it must be remembered that it is from these we hope to recruit our teaching staff. Of course, above all we teach the Bible stories and simple Christian doctrine. There is generally a special course of lessons for Christian children. We charge no fees at all in our schools. I am sometimes inclined to wonder whether natives might not value our teaching more if they paid a trifle for it. It would probably lessen our numbers, but this might be compensated by increased earnestness of those who persevered. On the whole, I should prefer to go on with our present system in this Mohammedan district. The Scotch and Dutch Reformed Missions charge school fees, and I am told that it works well. I only know by actual experience the work of the United Free Church of Scotland, and the education side of their work is wonderful. One of the staff told me that the school fees in the Bandawe district amounted to £70 in a single year, an amazing tribute to the intelligence of the natives of the district (Atonga) and still more to the good work of the missionaries. That was years ago, and doubtless the work has increased since then.

In these schools we have a constant supply of young people coming on towards baptism. Since the war our schools have been under a cloud in this Moslem district, where opposition is much stronger of late, but even here, though our numbers are small, we have recruits still coming on. For the elders we rely on village preaching, the influence of our medical work, and such personal influence as it is possible to bring to bear on them. When first people are attracted to our teaching they are written down as " hearers." They are under no promise, for as yet they are in no position to make one, for they do not know enough. They simply come to learn about Christianity. They have classes twice a week, to which the school children come, as well as adults, and also such patients as happen to be in hospital and are fit to come. They continue to hear for a period of from one to two years. By that time, if they have paid attention at classes, they know a little about Christianity. If they feel disinclined to accept Christianity, they can give it up without disgrace. If they really seek to become Christians, they are then definitely enrolled as catechumens. There is a short service in church; they make simple promises. When I can get them, I generally give a small brass cross to be worn round the neck. It is a reminder to themselves and it is also a protection, for every one in the village knows that there are things which those who have professed Christianity cannot do. As catechumens they can now come to a part of the service in church, but they sit behind a rail by themselves, not with the Christians. Like the hearers, they have their classes twice a week, but now it is a course of definite preparation for baptism. They are expected to come fairly regularly for two more years. It is regularity in attending the classes which is a great point when the time comes for choosing catechumens for baptism. This is not quite the mechanical test which it seems to be at first sight. To be regular and punctual is

not an easy thing for a native.   If one has come
regularly for two years, it is no bad sign that he
is really in earnest.

One of the chief causes of anxiety, before I
came to Africa, was the fear that I should be
horribly puzzled as to how to present Christianity to the heathen.   As one realizes that
these poor folk live in the bondage of fear, fear
of things physical, of witchcraft, of death—that
they have no hope for the future and only look
to grow up, and pass away in their old age into the
unknown darkness, through the awful doors of
mysterious death—one feels with a rush what
Christianity has to offer.   There are no doubt
many other avenues of approach, but one can
never be wrong in using this one.   One realizes,
perhaps, as never before the meaning of the
Light which came to lighten every man, for
native Africans indeed sit in darkness and the
shadow of death.

At last comes baptism, a day poignant with
hope and fear.   At any rate, one may practically
take it for granted that for the time at least
the candidates are in deadly earnest.   They are
clad in a white robe, marked with a scarlet cross.
They assemble with their godparents in the
catechumens' part of the church.   They have
been carefully taught the meaning of the promises and they make them solemnly enough.-
Then follows the rite, the men first and then

A MOTHER AND BABY.

the women. The priest then moves to the catechumens' barrier and admits them one by one into the congregation of Christ's flock, and they pass on to take their place with their Christian brethren. I wish I could describe what it means to the missionary priest. He has worked and prayed for these new Christians for so long. The day has come when he sees his work crowned. But behind his thankfulness there is the knowledge of all that lies before them, amongst the awful temptations of an African village. They are admitted Christ's soldiers and servants, and it is a grim fight indeed before them.

Lastly I come to the church. We follow native custom as far as possible. There are no seats. The people sit on large mats. Also the men sit on one side and the women on the other, just as they would do naturally in the village. The native tongues lend themselves admirably to music, for all vowels are long and all syllables are open, none end with a consonant. Central Africans are very much at home in church. The mothers bring their babies. If these infants are taken with a peculiarly noisy fit of screaming, they are taken outside to be comforted. Punctuality is not a strong point, and people go in and out in a very casual manner. Of course, this is not very desirable but at least there is no question, they feel at home in their

Father's house. Also they are all bare-footed and move very deftly, so there is no distressing clatter. There is a sung Eucharist every Sunday and Holy Day at 7 o'clock. That is the principal service of the day and there is a sermon. Immediately after this comes the catechumens' class. My native deacon takes this, while we hungry Europeans must needs have breakfast. At about half-past nine Mattins follow. My fellow padre, or the deacon, or my great stand-by, my lay brother—a licensed Lay-Reader—takes this service. I am engaged taking the hearers' class under a big tree. The regular hearers attend and odd people from the village come and listen. We have an English evensong and address at 4.15, followed immediately by native evensong. We have a daily Eucharist in English, except on Thursdays when it is in the native tongue, and a daily Mattins and evensong also for the natives. Besides these services we have daily sext and compline in English. On Fridays we have a sung native Litany, just at the close of school—a very popular service. These arrangements have to be broken into from time to time, especially where there is but one priest. He is bound to be away frequently to minister to the out-stations. But in spite of this drawback I think we may be thankful for our church privileges. My fellow missionaries will, I'm sure, agree with me that it is in the church and before the altar that we find the centre of our work and that it is there we get strength and inspiration to carry us through.

VI

Medical Work

THE medical work is a very important part of our organization. Our Master's own example in the first place consecrates all such work. It is also the one concrete example of what we mean by Christian charity, which cannot be misunderstood. I think that both these points should be kept in view. It is a very pitiful thing to see sick or maimed people in this country. The natives have little or no idea of nursing, though I'm sure they do their best, and every sort of discomfort is added to that of illness. One sees poor emaciated creatures lying on a mat on the hard floor, with no blanket or pillow, though often a kinsman will support the aching head upon his knee. The only invalid diet which they know is a washy sort of gruel that looks most uninviting. It is not only in serious illness that they are to be pitied. They know nothing of the body and a touch of fever, or even a bad cold, which can make one feel horribly ill, makes them think that they are in great danger and is apt to prostrate them utterly. For the same reason they will often neglect a serious illness which does not happen for the moment to cause them acute discomfort. Moreover, here at Mponda's, there are cases of crocodile wounds with terrible frequency. I cannot think how people ever get away when once gripped by those horrible jaws. But they do, and then the terrible wounds almost always become septic, even when no bones are broken. How should a poor soul treat a horrible septic wound in the village? A man must be hard-hearted indeed, if he does not long to help these poor things in their sickness. Then there is the other point. In helping such one is surely preaching the Gospel as words alone never will. I may preach and teach, but at the back of his mind the native thinks, I believe, that after all it is my business, an odd one to be sure, but doubtless there is some advantage behind it. When they see the nurses spending themselves to allay their pain, strangers, too, who seek no reward, it must indeed be a wonderful thing. Think, too, what it means in this Moslem district. There are no Mohammedan hospitals. The sick Moslem may have jeered at the Mission when in health. He comes humbly enough for help when sick, and it must make a great impression on him—as indeed I know that it does.

F.

We have unfortunately but one doctor in the diocese, attached to the Mission. His head-quarters are at Likoma, but he goes round to the other stations as often as possible. On some stations we are fortunate enough to be within reach of Government doctors. We, at Mponda's, owe a great debt of gratitude to successive Government doctors stationed at Fort Johnston. They have constantly shown themselves glad to help us—whether Europeans or natives. It was the same during the war. The military doctors were extraordinarily kind to us. I certainly owe my own life to the kindness of a doctor in the King's African Rifles. But, while we are so lucky in this way, other stations are out of reach of a doctor. It would seem as if we ought to have at least one other, especially as the doctor is bound, like other people, to take his leave from time to time.

This lack of doctors leaves the nurses with very heavy responsibilities. I have avoided all personalities as far as possible, but I cannot forbear to say how fortunate the Mission has been in its nurses, ever since I have known the diocese, and we have every reason to be proud of them. It is a matter of profound thankfulness that this should be so, for the work makes great demands upon them. We need not only nurses of high professional skill, but we need those who are missionaries at heart, and more, those who have the gift of getting on well with natives and inspiring them with confidence. For one so gifted there is an almost unlimited scope of usefulness in Nyasaland. One is glad to think that such work is going on at all our stations. Everywhere the old prejudice against European treatment has broken down. No one hesitates to seek our help in serious cases. A patient grievously torn by a crocodile is brought straight to our surgery, and the most painful treatment is submitted to with confidence. Only the other day I saw an amusing instance of this confidence. One of our local chiefs, as I happen to know, is very hostile to Europeans. He is naturally a Moslem, Mohammedanism being regarded as the native religion as against Christianity, the foreign religion. He is therefore much set against the Mission and once prevented me from opening a school in one of his dependent villages, where the people were really keen on having one. However, a violent earache brought him a humble suppliant to the Mission and I watched him meekly submitting to the English nurse's treatment, with some amusement. I hear that the treatment was entirely successful. I wonder if it will make any difference in his attitude to the Mission.

The nurses have native dressers under them. One or more is being trained on every station.

I am told that these boys are very useful and that one at least is really clever. Whether we shall be able to train our boys to attain to still higher qualifications remains to be seen. As it is, this part of the work must be not a little interesting.

In a short time we hope to have permanent hospitals, that is of brick or stone, on every station. These are generally plain buildings with a fire-place and a cement floor. At Mponda's we now have iron bedsteads strung with palm-leaf rope. We have room for twenty-two or twenty-three men. Our new women's hospital was begun as soon as post-war conditions allowed. The war came just as we were about to begin it, and it has been waiting ever since. I shall be very thankful to see our women patients better housed. The surgery, which is close by, should also be a better building when funds permit. This is crowded every morning and evening with patients of all sorts. I suppose that the characteristic ulcerated sore is far the commonest complaint.

There is no fixed fee, and no serious case is ever sent away, but the patients are expected to bring some form of offering. Sometimes they bring pennies, sometimes chickens or eggs. Others bring a bunch of corn-cobs or millet. The Indian traders are often patients at the surgery, and they always seem very grateful and gladly make a substantial offering. I always feel rather sorry for these exiles. I once let one of them have some milk, when he was sick, and his gratitude was quite overwhelming.

All this work must be having a profound influence. It will not show all at once. Every year is making our medical work better known and more appreciated throughout the district. Often, going through some strange village, I am hailed by some one whom I recognize as an old hospital patient. He invariably sends his salaams to the nurse. It is a case of casting bread on the waters, we do not see immediate results, but it must certainly bring a rich harvest some day.

VII

Travelling

A LARGE part of a missionary's life, especially if he be a priest, is spent in travelling. If there were no other reason, he is bound to go round his out-stations at least once a month to celebrate for his Christians. Where there are few or no Christians as yet, as is the case on newly-opened out-stations, the teacher and his wife have special claims on us in their isolated position, and have a right to expect reasonable opportunities of making their communions at least. But this is not the only reason. One ought to keep in touch, as far as possible, with these outlying parts. Africans have not the same staying powers as Europeans in methodical work, and one must do what one can to encourage them. I do not mean that they always get slack and lazy, but a teacher is apt to get discouraged at times, especially among these difficult Mohammedans in our own Yao district. Also there are cases cropping up continually with which the teacher cannot deal and which he must refer to his "padre." These are often unpleasant enough to deal with, but they only get worse if one's visit is delayed. I know nowhere where the policy of grasping the nettle is more important than in Africa. You may take it for granted that all troubles which are not met and dealt with at the earliest opportunity grow worse in the meantime.

A journey in Africa is not like a journey in England. In the first place you will generally have to walk. In the next place you will find no accommodation at the journey's end, except a bare roof to cover you. Everything you want you must take with you. African food does not suit an English stomach. It would make things much easier in every way if it did. As it is you cannot get food on the way, except such raw materials as eggs and chickens—or fish, if it be by the lake. You may also get African sweet potatoes and pumpkins in their season, and at times bananas. Some people generally take a tent. I never do myself. It means at least two more loads and those heavy ones. I trust to hiring a native house or sleeping in the Mission school. At worst I have slept in the open, but I confess to being a bit of a coward, and I don't like it. A fire burns down so quickly and, if one is asleep, one does not notice it, and I admit that,

when the fire burns down, I am a little shy of
creatures. There still remain quite enough
things to carry, without a tent. One needs
quite a staff of men for one's journey—"ulendo,"
as it is called by black and white alike, all
through Nyasaland.

I generally manage with four carriers. The
first carries the heaviest load, a tin box. In
this box I carry a change of clothes and such
matters, and also my church things. It should
be fairly water-tight, or you will have a sorry
time in the rains. It should not be very big,
not too big for a one-man load. It should be
provided with a lock. You may want to send
your loads on ahead and in any case you cannot
always be sitting on it, and it is really important
to have your money safe. Even if you are one
of those careless people, who do not seem to
mind the loss, and are rich enough to replace
the Mission money yourself, you have no sort
of right to put temptation in the way of weak
vessels, to whom a few shillings, or even a few
pence, seem riches. Number two carries a
bed bag, with a light camp-table, an " X
table " I always use. You will need blankets
in the cool season, both above and below. The
damp cold comes through a canvas bed in a
very distressing manner, and a native hut does
not keep this damp cold out as a solid house
does. You must also take a mosquito net.

Even on these rare occasions, when there seem to be no mosquitoes about, you should put it up, unless you want bats flapping in your face or noisome insects falling on you from the roof. Once I got in late and very tired, and I did not bother to put up the net. A scorpion fell from the roof, and got me, too. Of course, it was quite dark and I couldn't think what had happened. I thought I had touched some fire. I hastily struck a match, with tingling finger, and caught sight of the beast running for its life. It escaped, moreover, somewhere in the blankets and I expected more trouble, but I was too tired to search and, as a matter of fact, nothing further happened. Your bed-bag should have a bar lock. That does not prevent a reckless thief, for he merely slits the canvas, as happened to me once at Zomba, and I lost two beautiful new blankets. But it does stop your boys borrowing them, if you send your loads on a day ahead. I feel rather selfish in cold weather, but I do not like having my blankets borrowed, or even the thought of it. Number three carries a camp-bed, an " X bed," tied up with a chair. This sounds rather luxurious, but it would not do so to any one who knows the insect life of Africa. Unless you want ants crawling into the corners of your eyes and mouth while you are asleep, take a camp-bed. There are also worse than ants, ah! how much worse—but I will draw a veil. Happily, these creatures generally seem loath to climb a camp-bed, unless, for your sins, you are sick and have to lie there for some length of time. Number four carries the commissariat. Now this needs thought, for except an earthen cooking-pot, you can get nothing to help you in the village. A native cooking-pot, too, is, to say the least of it, greasy. When I once forgot to take any sort of vessel in which to boil water, I made shift with a cigarette tin. I made tea, in three boilings, and even boiled two tiny African eggs, or rather my boy did, but even he seemed to find it awkward, though he plays recklessly with live coals in his bare hands with impunity as a rule. You must be careful then to take a kettle, a pot, a frying pan and a teapot, and also crockery. Neither must you forget tea, sugar, salt and such. The house-keeper here is good enough to put up my food basket for me when I go travelling, and it is rare to find anything short. Over the top of the basket go two washhand basins, one for the ordinary purposes of a wash, and the other for the kitchen department. For a bath there are convenient streams on my own journeys. But besides these four carriers, you must have a cook. He generally acts as overseer or " kapi-tao " of the whole caravan. He cannot be expected to wash up and do odd jobs, so you must take a boy, too. My house-boy always goes with me and he is just a school-boy. His business also is to carry the hurricane lamp. In a country where the sun always sets about six o'clock a lamp is highly important, especially if you have to sleep without a door, as one often does in Mission schools. I always hope that a little light in the doorway will scare away wild beasts, but I should feel rather more comfortable at times if I felt sure of this.

Another thing to consider is that all these folks must have food, " posho " as it is called. When there is plenty of food about, it is simple enough. One just gives them a penny a day, according to the length of the journey, with something over. Then they do well enough. In times of scarcity you must take food with you, which means adding to your numbers. But, at whatever cost, never run the risk of being unable to feed your carriers. That is the deadly sin of " ulendo " work. You can go short at a pinch yourself, for you have no load to carry. They cannot, or even if they can, and they are wonderfully plucky, they ought not to have to do so. You will need simple medicines and quinine for yourself. I always take a flask of brandy with me. Natives are subject to fearful attacks of colic, especially in the green maize season. A little brandy seems to put them right. Let not the astute reader smile and think that the wily carrier has only to feign a stomach-ache to get brandy out of the simple missionary. It has only happened four or five times in fifteen years, but when it does happen, you may want it badly. I was once miles away from anywhere in the bush and one of my carriers went down with colic. The rest had gone on and we were all by ourselves. I felt in a most unpleasant fix. · However, a dessertspoonful of brandy allayed the trouble and, after a rest, the plucky fellow went on. I couldn't have carried the load myself half a mile. I was thankful indeed for the brandy then.

When I go to my more distant out-stations, I always send my loads off the day before. The walk by oneself next day through the forest is wonderfully interesting. One meets all sorts of people on the path, and they love to pass a word or two. I am something of a gossip and enjoy these chats. There are all sorts of birds and beasts to be seen. One sees antelopes occasionally. Once one nearly ran into me. As I said before, the country is very beautiful. I love wandering along alone, at one's own pace, enjoying the real Africa, far from everything that ever smacks of Europe. I am glad to say that I have only twice seen dangerous beasts, for I never bother to carry a rifle, and they appeared at least as anxious to avoid me as I was to avoid them. In each case it was a crafty-looking leopard, who stole across the path, crouching low, and, seeing me, bolted again into the bush. Of course, I speak of daytime. I do not go wandering about at night without a rifle.

When one arrives at one's destination there is plenty to do. After a rest and a cup of tea, a good many cups in the hot weather, there are various troubles to consider, which the teacher comes to report. It may be necessary to call several people if it be a subject that needs talking out. The sick must needs be visited, if there be any. The school must be looked at and perhaps examined. It may be well to hold a village·preaching. The space near the chief's house is generally the best place and evening the best time. Nearly always enough people will collect to listen, if only to look at a European, to examine his boots and his clothes. Anyway, there are always children. It is a very moving scene in the dusk. There are the children nearest, the boys not in the least shy, the girls rather more timid and a little further off. Then there are the ordinary grown up people, and amongst them a few poor old creatures. One thinks how much they need the message and how it might brighten their lives. One longs to know the right word which might touch a chord in their hearts.

Before one leaves there is the Eucharist in the early morning. Often it is in a tiny building, and it is but a small flock that gathers round. But we plead the one, all-sufficient sacrifice, just the same that is being offered in all the splendid churches of Christendom.

I should add that it is very important to be polite to the chief. I am on terms of friendship with all the chiefs in the villages where I have work. I am really fond of most of them, though one or two of them are rather tiresome people. I am sure that it is a duty to show them respect. When young men reach such a pitch of culture that they can read and write, they are apt to look down on their elders. Such things are known even in England. This is not only very bad for our Christian youths, but it is also very bad policy. The missionary then ought to show all due respect to the responsible ruler of the village. It is right that he should, and it will help the younger generation. I hope our Christians will win influence in the village by strength of character and by being good citizens of their small community. I do not want them to be a tiresome anarchical element in village life. It is well to give the chief a small prize occasionally. I only give two or three shillings myself. I don't want him to think that it is his interest to have boys at school, merely for the sake of presents.

In that case he would just send a few slave-boys. Of course, I should be glad enough to get them, but I want the others, too, who will some day have all the influence of free men in the village.

A missionary must expect a few discomforts on his travels, but now that all able-bodied men have experienced war service, these should seem small enough. The wet weather is certainly unpleasant. A native path, through tall, wet grass, is rather dreary, if one has many miles to plod. It is also very unpleasant if one has no opportunity of drying one's things and one has to put on wet boots and clothes again for next day's tramp. It is tiresome, too, if one goes sick, especially if one be far away. But when all is said, an "ulendo" is a pleasant change and is certainly nothing for an active body to worry about.

VIII

Native Christians

NOW it is a fair question to ask, What sort of Christians do native Africans make? ´ I can only answer that in many ways they are very unsatisfactory. But this answer does not cover the ground. One must ask further, What do you expect? Now to that question I should answer without hesitation that they are a great deal better than I should have expected. One must consider that they are the first, or in·a few places the second, generation of Christians. That means that the whole background of their lives, their villages and the customs in which they live are heathen or Mohammedan. One must remember that a sense of guilt before God is a new lesson and one hard to learn. They live very much in the present and are little awed by the prospect of future punishment. They have to learn that God wants a pure heart that a man may rise from his fallen state to be God's own loved child and may find his highest happiness in the beauty of holiness—which is God. That God is justice as well as love is another lesson difficult to learn. Of course, the native Christian has been taught all this, but it is only partly assimilated. Now it is difficult to build up a Christian character until these foundations have been laid. He is in process of assimilating, but in the meanwhile the Christian character is only in the process of being built up. Take away the knowledge of these things from us, or suppose we were only beginning to assimilate them, should we be likely to be startling examples of the work of grace ?

Again, I wonder how many of us can form any adequate conception of the temptation in which they live. One would be appalled at the idea of submitting a pure-minded English boy or girl to such temptation. In the war one saw only too sadly how fatal these temptations were to many a white man, with a thousand years of Christianity behind him. As I sit in my room at night, I can often hear the drums at four or five different beer-drinkings, going on at the same time. There I know is drunkenness and orgies, euphemistically called "dances," and many other deeds of darkness. The noise only bores you and me. , To my native boy it is about the only form of amusement he knows. He knows what the particular rhythm implies.

He knows that probably his kinsfolk are there·
Also the wretched rub-a-dub-dub is music
to him and brings to his mind a picture of a
bravely burning fire, of laughter and good cheer
—and the vice, ell, he is only just getting a
firm hold of the fact that it is vice at all.   Add
also the natural impulse to follow the crowd,
even stronger here than it is in England.
Nor does any one, least of all in youth, find it
easy to bear ridicule and the jeers at the odd
European teaching that would fain ban the
brave old customs of his fathers. Do you
wonder if he sometimes fall ?   I don't.

Then there is the marriage question.   His
brothers, his father, his uncles, all his clan have
married several wives and changed them again
as often as it seemed good to them.   His own
mother has haply had three or four husbands
in her time and likely enough all are still alive.
He is in process of learning that this is wrong
and of learning of the love that is but one,
that ideal union between man and wife, which
is even a type of the union between the Divine
Son of God and his Church.   He is learning,
good lad, but how when the sudden pinch comes,
the first serious quarrel of his married life ?
I don't know which is in fault, but both honestly
think it is the other.   The girl runs off home.
He has perhaps struck her and she is trembling
with pain and indignation.   She shrieks insults

at him, that she has done with him, that he had better seek another. Bitter wrath rises in his heart as he hears her insults. Even then there would be hope, but a crowd of jeering onlookers tell him to be a man and not to stand it. Others are telling the girl to show a proper spirit. And, ah me, how they talk all the time, for the African has the gift of tongues, as I verily believe no other race has. Do you wonder that they find it hard to forgive one another all at once, and are apt, at any rate until the exasperation has had time to wane a little, to make other unions, just to show their independence, unions which in the eyes of all their non-Christian kinsfolk are just as good and just as respectable as the marriage made in church ? They know that we say it is wrong. In calm moments they too know that it is wrong. But it is not burnt into them as it has been burnt into us and ours for centuries.

Then there is the question of dishonesty. In the village if a man gets into trouble because he will not tell a lie, people merely think what a blockhead he must be. Everybody lies, in private life or in the court, and everybody takes it for granted. As I said before, the African is a born actor. If he wants to do so, no Miltonic Belial could lie more sweetly. It is the same with stealing. I once heard a casual conversation in a village thirty-five miles away. The whole group were laughing over and unquestionably admiring the amazing performances of a transcendent thief. What was my horror to find that the hero was a Christian, a boy of one of my villages here! He was a boy whom I had baptized myself, the pity of it! Not that I was under any delusions about that young man. I knew long before that he was a heartbreaking failure. But I did not know that he was a popular hero, just as really as Robin Hood was to our own ancestors and without his excuses. Do you wonder that it takes time to drive home into African hearts the beauty of honesty?

But if African Christians are sadly apt to fall, albeit under the most grievous temptation, they are also apt to repent. When their conscience honestly condemns them, when they have had time to think calmly over things, they do most sincerely repent. The best thing is to walk in the straight path, but, if one has erred, the next best thing is to turn and repent. Even those who have tied themselves up in a permanent state of sin, say a bigamous marriage, are by no means filled with fierce hostility towards God and the Church, which must needs cast them out. They look back wistfully enough. They grieve that they can meet no more in the congregation of their Christian brethren. No, they have not the strength often enough to

break the bonds of their sin, but they half long
to do so. I had such a case only a while ago.
We had here an elder of the Church (or church-
warden) who, after long faithfulness married
bigamously, not without serious provocation
from his real Christian wife. He knew he was
wrong. He used to look bitterly ashamed of
himself when I chanced to meet him. He
grieved, I am sure of it, over his position.
Then he was stricken down by influenza and
soon it became clear that death was at hand.
As I knelt by him he gasped out what seemed
to be penitence, but he was almost inarticulate.
I shall never forget the scene. He lay in an
untidy hut. He was dripping wet, for in native
ignorance he had had cold water poured over
him to allay the burning fever. He was in
agony of body, but I am sure that he was in
greater agony of mind. The wistful look on
his face, as he tried to make me hear, wrung
one's heart. He was a mission failure, I suppose,
but I still hope and I dare not condemn.

I admit that there are many failures amongst
our African Christians, but there are also many
penitents. On the whole, however, I am
convinced, as I said before, that they are
better than one would expect. Do Europeans
never fail ? Moreover, there are, thank God,
some at least who are of the salt of the earth.
Also there are many, many who in spite of all

temptations, in spite of being of the first generation of Christians, in spite of all, live pure and honest lives. They are, perhaps, not of the most deeply spiritual sort, but they are faithful. Indeed, I believe that in serious temptation, even in cruel persecution, they would still be faithful. To me African Christians are wonderful. Even if they were far, far worse, it would but give point to the old prayer, " Come over and help us."

IX

The Missionary

WHEN one is trying to decide whether one is called to missionary work, I am assuming in this case in Central Africa, there are certain things which I feel one ought to know. It is true that they are mostly obvious enough. One might easily guess them at home, but somehow one doesn't.

The first consideration is health. I put it first, for it is the one that weighs most with one's friends. I take it that if a body is not reasonably strong he will regard this as a perfectly clear intimation that his work does not lie in an exacting climate in tropical Africa. But so much is talked at home about that awful scourge, malaria, that even the strongest begins to think that it is little short of martyrdom to come out to Africa at all. As a matter of fact, an ordinary attack of malaria is not a very serious business. I speak, of course, as a layman, not as a doctor, but I am sure that a doctor would say the same. The fever runs its course and one lies in bed till it is over, and then one feels all right again. Nor does it leave one in the prostrate condition which influenza does, unless one gets a succession of fevers, but that is no more common than any other serious illness at home. For my own part, I have felt just as wretched with a heavy cold at home as I have ever felt with a fever in Africa. I admit that I am one of the lucky ones. Headache is, I suppose, the worst part of fever, but I have never had a headache in my life. Still, folks who have headaches with fever no doubt have headaches with colds at home. Certainly there are other tropical diseases which are bad enough—dysentery, blackwater fever and tick-fever—but these one does not expect to get. Malaria, such as it is, you are pretty sure to get. In spite of all precautions, there are few who get through the first two years without it.

This brings me to such precautions as one ought to take. I am convinced that it ought to be a serious matter of conscience to obey the medical rules. You will sometimes meet people who jeer at quinine. They say that they never have fever and they don't touch quinine. There are, no doubt, a few peculiarly constituted in this respect, just as there are other sorts of freaks. Also, no doubt, medical science has still much to learn. Still, the broad fact remains that after careful research in all parts of the world, covering millions of individuals, scientific men have arrived at certain conclusions and give us certain advice. The soundness of their teaching has been proved by the almost miraculous change which it has brought in tropical countries. Such as it is, it is the best advice we have, and for a layman to jeer at it seems to be mere conceit. God has given us only one life, and we have no right whatever to throw it away. Nor ought one to take foolish and unnecessary risks. It is surprising how reckless otherwise sensible people can be. I once knew a bishop, no less, who shall be nameless, who got soaked to the skin, clad in white drill, and he was not for taking the trouble of changing his clothes. It was warm and he said he didn't mind. I worried him till he went and changed, but he did it a thought resentfully. There are times when one must take risks, just as anywhere else, and in that case there is nothing more to be said. I was once sent for to baptize a catechumen who was suddenly taken ill. He lived more than a mile away and it was pouring with heavy, tropical rain. I was myself suffering from dysentery, though I didn't know it. Of course, I had to go. But to have taken that walk for nothing would surely have been criminal.

When I first thought of coming out here the thing I most dreaded was the appalling isolation, as it seemed to me. Not only would one be away from one's friends, but from the world, its interests, its politics and everything that goes to make up civilization. Now one must grant that one misses books. That is a really serious deprivation. But even so one can have a certain number of books sent out to one, and one can get books from the diocesan library at Likoma, though seldom of the latest. For the rest I found isolation almost as much a bugbear as fever. I don't know if I unconsciously regarded natives as things, as machines. To my astonishment I found them human, I found myself in a new world, a real-live place full of human interests. Mponda's village has about the same population as my own little town in Derbyshire, and it is just as full of all manner of interests, indeed in some ways fuller, for one comes on so much that is new and unexpected. As soon as one gets a little over the language difficulty there need be no fear of isolation. Could anything at home equal such a drama as this, at any rate in pre-war days ? I once sat under a tree by the lake-side and listened to the story of a raid which had taken place while I was away on leave. The narrator was one of the warriors who had taken part in the defence. As he sat he pointed to the places of interest in the story. It was like a passage of Homer, except that it was full of close personal interest, not a long-told tale. The teller's voice vibrated with emotion at each crisis of the story. He began in anxious tones to describe the searchings of heart in his own village when they heard shots and saw the flames in the next village, a kindred village of their own. His tone became firmer as they resolved on pursuit. It rang in triumph as he told of the victorious fight. It fell again almost into a minor key as he told of the dead, and especially of a poor woman speared by her brutal captor when he found that there was no escape. It is true that one does not often come upon exciting incidents like this, but nor does one meet them in England, or did not in pre-war days. No, there is far too much human interest in an African village. One need not be isolated. Also, while entering into this new world, one does not really lose touch with the old. One gets newspapers; albeit six or seven weeks late at least. But there is no vital necessity that a man must lose interest in affairs if he does not get the news next morning. Were English people bored with the news of Waterloo because it did not come for a fortnight after the battle? I think that I take as much interest in politics, home or foreign, as ever I did, except that 'from this distance home politics often look rather petty, but that may be really a juster view. I read of religious and social questions as eagerly as ever I did. Nay, even at my age, I still rejoice when Oxford wins a boat race or when St. John's goes up a place on the river. When on leave last year I watched Oxford's interesting victory at Lords with much the same feelings as I watched a 'varsity match twenty years ago. I am sure no one need fear becoming an isolated fossil out here. If he does become one he is the sort of man who would have become a fossil in London or Paris.

When a man comes to Africa he must expect to meet with difficulties. In the first place there is the language. Neither Chi-Nyanja nor Yao are hard as languages go, I think, but they must be learnt. Moreover, the European will never have done learning. Behind the language there is a still greater difficulty, and that is to get at the point of view of the native. The background of his life is so different from ours. All his customs and ways of looking at life are new to us. However, half the danger is gone if a man is sensible and knows when he doesn't know. Nor when one makes a mistake must one lose heart, for one meets difficulties everywhere. If we were to lose heart there is no one else out here to take our place. Also, every year will bring fuller knowledge and fuller usefulness to the man who humbly tries to do his best.

Every man must decide for himself in the last resort as to what he believes to be God's will, but I am sure that if in the end he finds that his lot is cast in Africa he will find it a fair place. All he can do, with his head or his hand, all he has ever learnt, will come in useful here. Here, too, he will find the battle well-defined, and will see his duty plain before him as one seldom can among the puzzling questions at home. He will find it a good country to live in. I will go further, for I know something of death in Africa. If it be good for a man that death should find him following God's calling with a stout heart, then I say that Africa is also a good country to die in.

Printed in Great Britain by Butler & Tanner, *Frome and London*

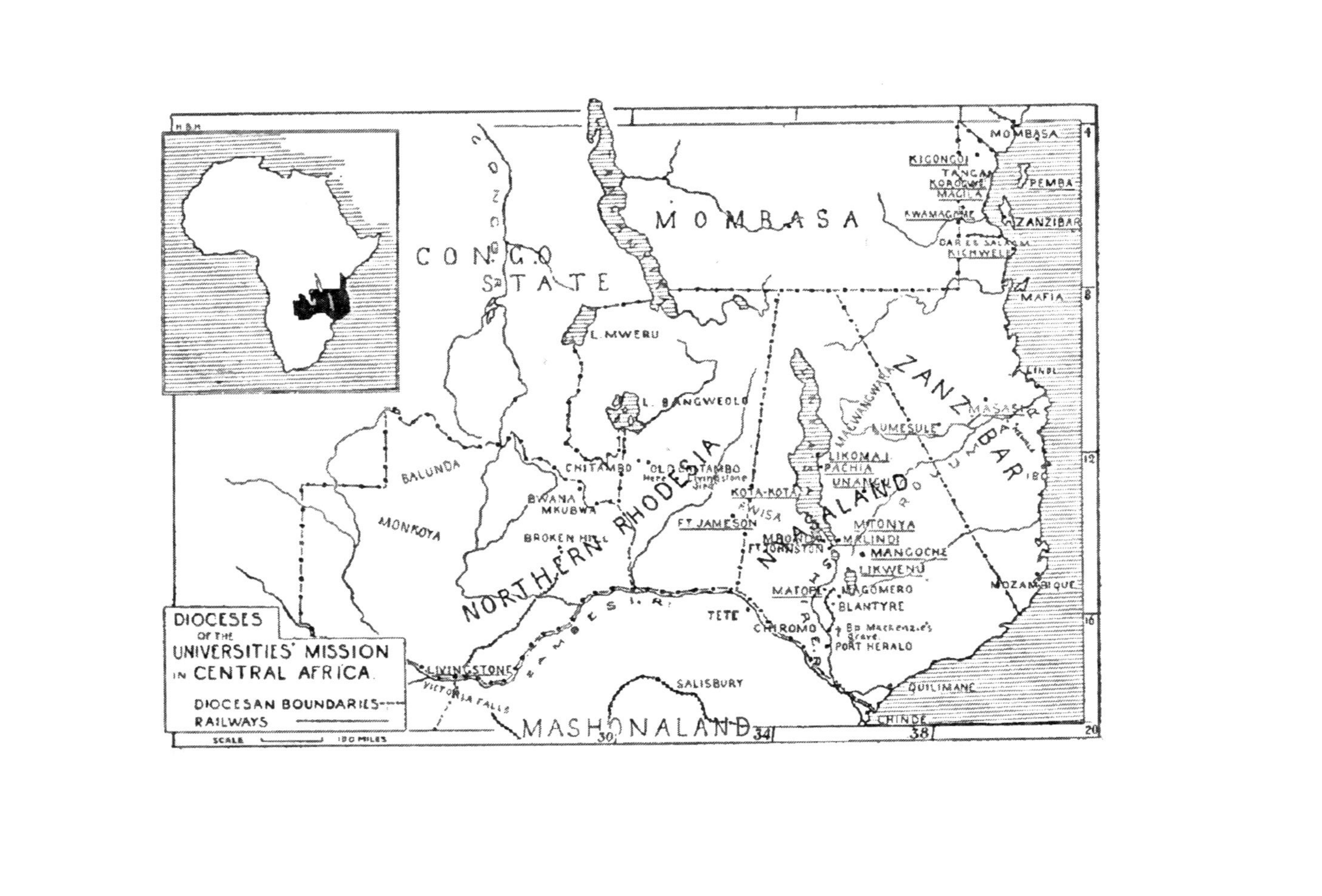

DIOCESES
OF THE
UNIVERSITIES' MISSION
IN CENTRAL AFRICA
DIOCESAN BOUNDARIES
RAILWAYS
SCALE
100 MILES
MOMBASA
CONGO STATE
ZANZIBAR
NORTHERN RHODESIA
NYASALAND
MASHONALAND
MOMBASA
KIGONGOI
TANGA
KOROGWE
MAGILA
KWAMAGWE
ZANZIBAR
PEMBA
DAR ES SALAM
KICHWELE
MAFIA
LINDI
MASASI
UMESULE
NEWANGWARA
LIKOMA
PACHIA
UNANGU
LIKWENU
MTONYA
MALINDI
MANGOCHE
MAGOMERO
BLANTYRE
MATOPE
MBO
FT JOHNSTON
KOTA-KOTA
MWISA
FT JAMESON
OLD CHITAMBO
Here Livingstone died
CHITAMBO
BWANA MKUBWA
BROKEN HILL
BALUNDA
MONKOYA
L. MWERU
L. BANGWEOLO
TETE
CHIROMO
Bp Mackenzie's Grave
PORT HERALD
MOZAMBIQUE
QUILIMANE
CHINDE
ZAMBESI R.
SHIRE R.
LIVINGSTONE
VICTORIA FALLS
SALISBURY

Nela
Songea
Wikihi
Likoma
Kobwe
Ngoo
Msumba
Mtengula
Kota Kota
Unangu
Mtonya
Msinje
Lungwena
Monkey Bay
Mpondas
Malindi
Likwenu
Zomba

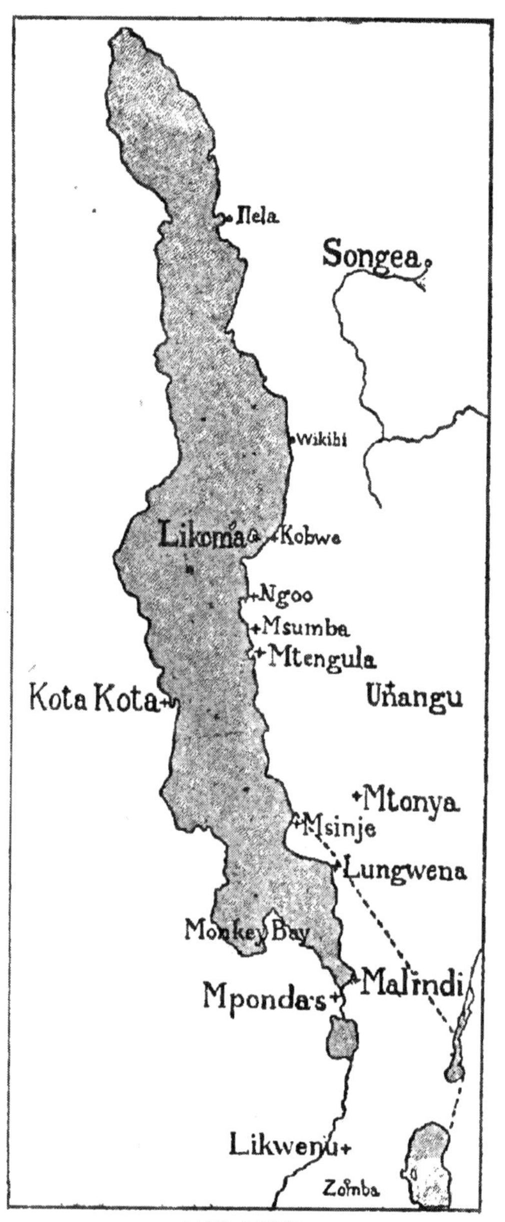

LAKE NYASA

. . **The** . .

Universities' Mission to Central Africa.

Proposed by Livingstone, 1857.   C. F. Mackenzie, First Bishop,
January, 1, 1861.

President—THE RIGHT REV. BISHOP GORE.

Head Office: 9 DARTMOUTH STREET, WESTMINSTER, S.W.1.

SPHERE.
Between the Equator in the North and the River Zambesi in the South.

DIOCESES.
Zanzibar, Nyasaland and Northern Rhodesia.

OBJECTS.
To free Africans from heathenism and Mohammedanism, to build up an African Church, to maintain schools and training colleges, teach handicrafts and nurse the sick.

NEEDS.
(*a*) More priests and lay workers to fill vacancies and for the extension of the work.

(*b*) A largely increased income to meet increased charges and the loss on exchange.

MAGAZINES.
"Central Africa" (**2d.**). "African Tidings" (**1d.**). Monthly.

SECRETARY.
Rev. CANON TRAVERS, U.M.C.A., 9 Dartmouth Street, Westminster, S.W.1.

Catalogue of publications sent free on request.

17-18 Chiefs

20   Ajacan — [illegible] action

22   patient [illegible] [illegible]
         [illegible]

23   [illegible]
         [illegible]

24   [illegible]

25   [illegible]
         forgetting

26   [illegible] & man who calls alone

27   [illegible]
         [illegible]

28   love & children — spirit [illegible]

29   [illegible]
         [illegible]

[illegible] Children [illegible]
         XI [illegible]

29   Training of [illegible]

31   Village [illegible]

34   Chieftain [illegible]

34   Custom [illegible]

35   [illegible]

40   [illegible]

II⁰ 40   "Whoever [illegible], he must be every
         [illegible]"

U